Love Conquers Death and Other Stories

A collection of tales from India
by Catherine Khoo and Marguerite Siek

Retold by F.H. Cornish

HEINEMANN

ELEMENTARY LEVEL

Series Editor: John Milne

The Heinemann Guided Readers provide a choice of enjoyable reading material for learners of English. The series is published at five levels – Starter, Beginner, Elementary, Intermediate and Upper. At **Elementary Level**, the control of content and language has the following main features:

Information Control
Stories have straightforward plots and a restricted number of main characters. Information which is vital to the understanding of the story is clearly presented and repeated when necessary. Difficult allusion and metaphor are avoided and cultural backgrounds are made explicit.

Structure Control
Students will meet those grammatical features which they have already been taught in their elementary course of studies. Other grammatical features occasionally occur with which the students may not be so familiar, but their use is made clear through context and reinforcement. This ensures that the reading as well as being enjoyable provides a continual learning situation for the students. Sentences are kept short – a maximum of two clauses in nearly all cases – and within sentences there is a balanced use of simple adverbial and adjectival phrases. Great care is taken with pronoun reference.

Vocabulary Control
At **Elementary Level** there is a limited use of a carefully controlled vocabulary of approximately 1,100 basic words. At the same time, students are given some opportunity to meet new or unfamiliar words in contexts where their meaning is obvious. The meaning of words introduced in this way is reinforced by repetition. Help is also given to the students in the form of vivid illustrations which are closely related to the text.

Contents

A Note About These Stories

India is the largest country in South Asia. The capital of India – the most important city – is Delhi. More than 850 million people live in India. These people have many different languages and religions. The official language of the country is Hindi but many people speak English.

Religion is very important to the people of India. Hinduism, Sikhism, Buddhism, Islam and Christianity are the most important religions. Most Indians are Hindus.

People have lived in India from about 3500 BC. In about 1500 BC, a group of people from Europe came to the north of the country. These people were the first Hindus. There are many gods in the Hindu religion. Different Hindus pray to different gods. Some people pray to Brahma who is a god of creation.

Two other gods who people pray to are Vishnu and Shiva. In Hindu stories, Vishnu sometimes comes to the Earth. Each time, he is born as a man. These great men do good things and they fight evil. The most famous of these men are Rama and Krishna. There are two very old books of stories about these two men – the *Ramayana* and the *Mahabharata*. The *Ramayana* is a collection of stories about Rama and other holy people. The *Mahabharata* tells about the life of Krishna. One of the stories in this book, 'Love Conquers Death', is from the *Ramayana*.

At first, there were many small kingdoms in India. But from AD 1526 to 1761, the Mughals ruled the land. They were strong rulers and they made many laws. Some very beautiful sculptures and paintings come from the time of the Mughals.

In later years, the British ruled India. The country became independent in 1947. At that time, a large area in the northwest of India became a new country – Pakistan. Most people in Pakistan are Muslims.

Indians come from four different groups of families. These are called castes. There were four castes. The members of the first caste were the *Brahmins*. They were priests or teachers. *Kshatriyas* were the second caste. They were great soldiers or rulers. The members of the third caste were *Vaishyas* – shopkeepers, traders or farmers. *Shudras* were the fourth caste. They were workers or servants.

India is a huge country. In the north are the Himalayas. These are the world's highest mountains. India's longest rivers, the Ganga (Ganges) and the Brahmaputra, start in the Himalayas and they go to the sea in the Bay of Bengal. The Ganga is a holy river to the Hindu people. In the northern and the southern parts of India there are thick forests of trees. Many animals live in these areas. But the centre of India is a great desert, a very dry land with many rocks and stones. It is very hot in this part of the country and very little rain falls there.

In these stories you will read about kings (*rajas*) who ruled small kingdoms long ago. They lived in fine palaces. They often fought with each other. Rajas had armies of soldiers to protect their lands and guards to protect their palaces. These kings had hundreds of attendants and servants. Advisers helped the rajas to rule their kingdoms.

The rajas and their families wore beautiful clothes and jewellery made of gold and precious stones – emeralds, rubies and pearls. Rajas and princes often went hunting in the forests. They rode horses and they caught elephants, tigers, antelopes and lions.

There are magicians in two of these stories. One of them is a good, kind man. He helps people with his magic powers. But the other magician is a wicked man. He tells lies to people and uses his magic powers to do evil things. He lives in a castle – a strong building made of stone.

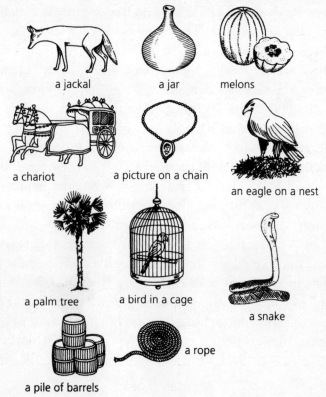

a jackal

a jar

melons

a chariot

a picture on a chain

an eagle on a nest

a palm tree

a bird in a cage

a snake

a pile of barrels

a rope

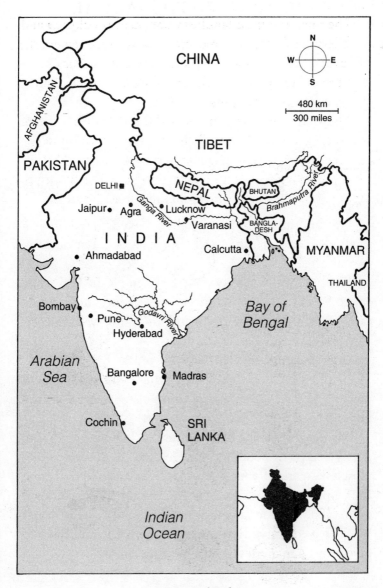

A Map of India

THE GIFTS OF THE JACKAL

1

The First Gift

A long time ago in India, there lived a *brahmin*. He came from a good family but he was very poor. The brahmin was an old man. His wife was dead, but he had seven pretty daughters.

The brahmin and his daughters lived together in a small wooden hut. They had a little garden, but nothing grew there.

The brahmin was very poor. Sometimes, he had a few coins. Sometimes, he had no money. Sometimes, people gave him food. But often, he and his family were hungry. The brahmin was always worried.

One evening, the old man looked at his daughters. They were tired and thin. Each of them had eaten a small piece of bread. There was nothing else to eat. And the brahmin had no money.

'My daughters,' the brahmin said. 'I don't know what to do. We have no food and we have no money. Someone must take care of you. Young girls get married and then their husbands take care of them. But no young men will marry you. If a young man wanted to marry one of you, I would have to give him a wedding-gift. I would have to give him some money. And I have no money!'

'I must find husbands for you, my daughters,' the old man went on sadly. 'If a dog or a jackal wants to marry one of you, you must agree to marry him. A dog or a jackal will not want a wedding-gift!'

The brahmin's seven daughters laughed. 'Girls do not marry animals, Father!' one of them said.

But at that moment, they heard a noise outside the hut. Then somebody knocked on the door. The brahmin got up and opened the door.

A jackal walked into the hut. The jackal had a bag in its mouth. He put the bag on the ground by the brahmin's feet. Then the jackal spoke.

'Dear sir,' the jackal said, 'I was walking past your hut. I heard your words. I can help you. This bag is full of gold. I will give you this bag of gold if I can marry one of your daughters.'

The old man did not know what to do. He was a brahmin, a person from a good family. He did not want one of his daughters to marry an animal. He did not want an animal to be his son-in-law. But he was very poor. He could buy food for all his family with this gold. He could buy enough food for many months.

He looked sadly at his daughters. At last he spoke.

'Who will marry this good jackal?' he said.

For a few moments, everyone was silent. Then the eldest girl spoke.

'Father,' she said, 'I will marry this good jackal. I will marry him tomorrow.'

———

The next morning, the jackal took his new wife to his home. They started to walk towards the hills.

The girl was worried.

'Jackals live in caves in the rocks,' she thought. 'A cave will not be a good place to live. At night, it will be colder than my father's hut.'

After an hour, the jackal and his wife came to a cave in a hillside. The jackal led the girl inside. They walked a long way into the cave.

At last, they came to a wooden door. The jackal opened the door.

'Come in,' said the animal kindly. 'This is your home now.'

The girl went through the door. She was very surprised. She was in a large, beautiful room – a room in a palace!

'My husband is not a jackal,' she thought. 'Who is he? Is he a prince? Am I asleep? Is this a dream?'

Then she looked at her husband.

'Yes, he *is* a jackal!' she thought. 'But my husband has a secret which he does not tell anyone.'

What was her husband's secret? When the jackal went out of the cave, the girl thought about it for a long time.

'I will not ask him about his secret,' she said to herself at last. 'One day, he will tell me who he is.'

———

'This is your home now,' said the jackal.

2

The Second Gift

For many months, the girl's father and her six sisters were happy. They had a good life. They bought food with the jackal's gold. But one day, there was no more gold in the bag. And soon there was no food for the family. The brahmin spoke to his daughters.

'I will go and visit my son-in-law, the good jackal,' he said.

The brahmin wanted the jackal to give him another bag of gold. But did not say that. He said, 'I am worried about your sister. Is the jackal taking care of her? I must go and see them.'

The next day, the brahmin went to find his daughter and her husband. The jackal saw him coming up the hill.

The jackal did not want his father-in-law to see the palace in the cave. So he went to meet the old brahmin on the hillside.

'My dear son,' said the brahmin. 'I am hot and tired. I will rest in your cave for a hour.'

'Please don't come into my cave,' said the jackal. 'It is cold and dark in there. Father, stay here, and I will call my wife. She will bring you some food and some water.'

The jackal went into the cave. He spoke to his wife.

'Please, don't tell your father our secret,' he said. 'Don't tell him about the palace in the cave.'

A few minutes later, the brahmin's eldest daughter

came out to see her father. She was beautiful! She was dressed in fine clothes. She brought some food and some water for the old man.

The brahmin's daughter talked to her father. But she did not tell him about her new life. She did not tell him about the palace in the cave. She asked him about her sisters. She listened to her father's news.

At last, the old man asked her, 'Are you happy, my daughter?'

'Yes, Father,' she replied, 'I am very happy. Now, what can I do to make *you* happy?'

'Daughter,' the old man replied. 'There is no more gold. We cannot buy food. Your sisters are hungry. Please, will you ask your husband to give me some more money?'

'Yes, Father, I will ask him,' she said.

And she went into the cave to find the jackal.

After a few minutes, the jackal came out of the cave. He was carrying a small bag. He gave the bag to the brahmin. It was not heavy. There was no gold in it!

'Father, I cannot give you any money,' the jackal said. 'But here is a bag of melon seeds. Take the seeds to your garden and put them into the ground. When the fruits grow, take them to the market and sell them. Then you will not be hungry. Goodbye, Father.'

The brahmin was not pleased with the jackal's gift.

'I wanted some gold, not a bag of melon seeds,' he said to himself. But he did not say this to his son-in-law. He thanked the jackal and he said goodbye.

That afternoon, the brahmin took the seeds into his

garden. Quickly, he planted them in the ground.

A few days later, the seeds had grown into melon plants. And many large, beautiful melons were growing on the plants.

The brahmin spoke to his neighbour. His neighbour was a fruit-seller. He sold fruit in the market.

'Look at these melons,' the brahmin said. 'Have you ever seen better melons?'

'Give me one of them,' said the fruit-seller. 'I will take it home and eat some of it. If it has a good taste, I will buy all your melons.'

So the brahmin picked a melon from one of the plants and he gave it to his neighbour. The fruit-seller took it home.

The fruit-seller got a knife and he cut the melon in half. But when he looked inside the fruit, he was very surprised. It was full of precious stones! There were no seeds in the melon. There were rubies and emeralds and pearls!

The fruit-seller put the precious stones in a bag. Then he ran back to the brahmin's hut.

'Your melon had a very good taste,' he said. 'I will buy *all* your melons immediately.'

The brahmin was pleased. He and his six daughters picked all the melons in the garden. They gave them to their neighbour, and the fruit-seller gave the brahmin some coins.

'Now we can eat again,' the brahmin said. And the old man went to buy some food at the market.

———

Inside the melon, there were rubies and emeralds and pearls!

The next morning, there were many more fruits on the melon plants. Again, the brahmin and his daughters picked them. Again, they sold the melons to their neighbour. This happened for three more days. Then the melon plants died. There were no more fruits on them.

'I have no more melons,' the brahmin told his neighbour.

The fruit-seller now had many precious stones, but the brahmin had only a few coins. And soon, all the money had gone. Soon, the brahmin's family was hungry again.

'What shall we eat today, my daughters?' the brahmin asked one morning.

Two of the old man's daughters went into the garden. They found two very small melons on the ground.

'We will cook these two melons,' said one of the daughters. And the two girls went back into the hut to cook the fruit.

But when they cut the melons, they were surprised! The fruits had no seeds, but there were a few small emeralds and rubies and pearls inside them. The girls told their father about these precious stones.

'The fruit-seller has the stones from our large melons,' the brahmin said. 'He found precious stones in the melon which I gave him. He wanted to buy all the other melons. I will ask him for some of the stones.'

The brahmin went to see his neighbour.

'Dear friend,' he said. 'You paid us for ordinary melons. But those melons were *not* ordinary. They were extraordinary melons! They were full of emeralds and rubies and pearls. Please, give us some of the stones. We did not know about the stones when we sold the fruits to you.'

The fruit-seller became angry.

'You are mad, old man!' he shouted. 'Those fruits were ordinary melons. There were no precious stones in them. Go away, old man!'

Sadly, the brahmin went home. 'I have a few stones,' he thought. 'I will sell those. Then I can buy food for a few weeks.'

———

The next morning, the brahmin went to see a jeweller – a man who bought and sold precious stones. He went to the jeweller's shop in the market. He showed him the emeralds and the rubies and the pearls.

'You are a poor man,' said the jeweller. 'Where did you get these stones? Did you steal them? Did you steal them from my shop, old man?'

'No, no!' said the brahmin. 'I got them from my son-in-law. He gave them to me.'

'Is your son-in-law a rich man?' asked the jeweller. 'Is he a prince? These are fine stones.'

The brahmin was an honest man. He did not want to tell a lie to the jeweller. So he told him the truth.

'No, he isn't a prince,' he said. 'He's a jackal.'

'You are lying!' shouted the jeweller. 'Animals don't have precious stones! These are *my* stones! You stole them!'

And the jeweller called his friends. They came run-ning from the other shops in the market. The brahmin told them his story. But they did not believe him.

'You stole the stones from the jeweller,' they said. 'You must give the stones to him now or you will go to prison.'

So the brahmin gave his precious stones to the jeweller. Sadly, he walked home.

That night, the brahmin and his daughters had nothing to eat.

3

The Third Gift

The next morning, the brahmin went to see his son-in-law again. Again, the jackal met him on the hillside. The old man told the jackal his story. The jackal laughed.

'What an unlucky man you are, Father!' he said. 'But do not worry! I will give you another gift.'

The jackal went into his cave. When he came out again, he was carrying a large jar.

'This is not an ordinary jar, Father,' he said. 'It is a magic jar. When you are hungry, put your hand into this jar. You will always find food inside it. But this is a secret. You must not tell anybody about this jar. And you must not tell anybody about me!'

'Thank you, dear son,' said the old man. And he carried the jar back to his wooden hut.

For three months, the brahmin and his daughters had a good life. They ate good food every day. There was always food in the jar. And it was good, hot food. No one had to do any cooking!

Then one day, the brahmin was unlucky again.

The old man and his daughters were eating their meal when the *raja* and his guards went past the brahmin's hut. The raja was the ruler of the land where the brahmin lived. He was not a kind man. He was cruel.

The raja stopped outside the hut and said, 'I can smell food. Someone is cooking wonderful food. The smell is coming from that hut!'

The raja knocked on the door of the old man's hut. When the brahmin opened the door, the raja saw many dishes of food on the brahmin's table.

'That food has a wonderful smell,' said the raja. 'But you are a poor man. How can a poor man get good food?'

The brahmin forgot the jackal's words. He told the raja the secret of the magic jar.

The raja did not believe the brahmin's story. So the old man went to the jar and he put his hand into it. He took out some hot, cooked food. It had a wonderful smell!

Then the raja believed the old man's story. And he was hungry, so the brahmin gave him some of the food.

'Where did you get this magic jar?' the raja asked.

'My son-in-law gave it to me, sir,' the brahmin answered.

'Is your son-in-law a magician?' the raja asked.

'No, sir. He is a jackal,' the brahmin replied.

'Where did you get this magic jar?' the raja asked.

'You are lying, old man!' the raja shouted. 'Your son-in-law is not a jackal. Women do not marry animals! You have stolen this jar from a magician.'

The raja called his guards. They ran into the hut. The raja pointed at the brahmin.

'Hold that old man!' he shouted. 'He is a thief! Ask his neighbours if anyone has lost a magic jar.'

The guards spoke to the neighbours, but none of them had lost a magic jar.

At last, the raja told the guards to free the old man. Then the raja left the brahmin's hut. But he took the magic jar with him.

4

The Fourth Gift

The next day, the old man went to see his son-in-law again. Once more, the jackal met him on the hillside.

The jackal was angry. 'You did not remember my words!' he said. 'You told someone the secret of the jar. I will give you one more gift. But I will not help you again. You must not tell anyone else about me!'

The jackal went into his cave. Soon he returned with another jar.

'Take this jar, Father,' he said. 'In this jar there is a magic rope. There is also a magic stick. You can use them to punish bad men. When you say, "Rope and stick!", these things will jump out of the jar. Then you must point at the wicked man. The rope will tie itself round that person. And the stick will beat him. The stick will beat him until you tell it to stop.

'Go and visit the jeweller and the fruit-seller and the raja,' the jackal went on. 'Take the jar with you. Show them the rope and the stick. The wicked men will give you the things which they stole from you!'

The brahmin was very pleased. 'Thank you, dear son,' he said.

He took the jar and he walked back to his hut.

———

The next morning, the brahmin went to the raja's palace. He spoke to one of the raja's servants.

'I have a gift for the raja,' he said. 'I have another magic jar.'

Soon, the raja asked his servants to bring the brahmin to his room.

'What can *this* jar do, old man?' the raja asked.

'You will see!' the brahmin said. Then he shouted, 'Rope and stick!'

A rope and a stick jumped out of the jar. The old man pointed at the raja. The rope flew across the room and tied itself round the cruel ruler.

When the raja could not move, the stick flew across the room and began to beat him.

'Stop! Stop!' cried the raja.

'Give me my food jar,' said the brahmin. 'Then I will

tell the stick to stop beating you. And I will tell the rope to untie itself.'

A few minutes later, the brahmin left the raja's palace. He had the food jar in one hand and the rope-and-stick jar in the other hand. But he did not go home. He went to see his neighbour, the fruit-seller.

'Go away, old man,' the fruit-seller said.

'Rope and stick!' the brahmin shouted. He pointed at the fruit-seller. Soon, the rope had tied itself round the fruit-seller and the stick was beating him.

'Where are my precious stones?' the brahmin asked. 'If you tell me, I will tell the stick to stop beating you.'

'They are in that bag!' cried the fruit-seller. 'Take them and go away!'

So the brahmin took his stones and he went to the jeweller's shop.

'Go away, thief!' said the jeweller.

'Rope and stick!' shouted the brahmin. And soon he had the stones which the jeweller had taken from him.

———

Now the brahmin was a rich man. He and his daughters had a good life again. Now, he could give wedding-gifts to the young men who wanted to marry his daughters. And soon, his six younger daughters were married to fine young men.

The brahmin's eldest daughter was happy when she heard the news.

'At last, my father is lucky,' she said.

The brahmin's eldest daughter was happy. But she often

'Rope and stick!' shouted the brahmin.

thought about her husband's secret.

———

Every day, the jackal got up very early and he left the palace. He returned three hours later. One morning, his wife decided to follow him.

The jackal left the cave and he began to walk towards the mountains. The brahmin's daughter followed him. After an hour, they came to a big lake.

The jackal walked to the side of the lake and he took off his skin! At last his wife understood. He was *not* a jackal. He was a handsome young man!

The young man put the jackal's skin on the ground and he jumped into the lake. He started to swim in the cool water.

The brahmin's daughter had an idea. Quickly, she ran to the lake and she picked up the jackal's skin. Then she went home to the palace in the cave and she threw the skin onto a fire.

Later, the young man came home. He smiled at his wife. 'Now you know my secret!' he said.

'Who are you?' the brahmin's daughter asked him. 'Please tell me now.'

'I am a prince,' he said. 'And I am a magician. I changed into a jackal because I like to help people. But I do not want them to know who I am. When I am a jackal, I help people. And they do not know who I am.

'But now *you* know who I am. You have been a good wife. You loved me when I was a jackal. Will you love me when I am a prince again?'

'Yes,' said the brahmin's daughter, and she smiled at her husband. 'I will always love you.'

So the brahmin's seven daughters were all married to fine young men. And everyone lived happily for the rest of their lives.

THE WICKED MAGICIAN

1

Seven Brothers and Their Brides

Long ago, a king lived in India. He was a good king. He ruled his kingdom well and his people loved him.

The king had seven young sons.

There were many forests in the kingdom. The seven princes liked to go to the forests and hunt animals.

One day, the seven princes left their father's palace early in the morning. They rode on horses. They rode to a great green forest and they hunted all day.

When the sky began to get dark, the princes started to ride back to the palace. After an hour, the youngest prince stopped his horse.

'Brothers,' he said, 'can you hear someone crying? There is someone calling for help.'

The brothers listened. They all heard the sound.

'We must find the person who is calling,' said the youngest prince. 'Something is wrong. Someone is very unhappy.'

The seven brothers went on through the forest. Soon they came to a flat place between the trees. In this clearing, seven beautiful young women were sitting on the ground.

Six of them were crying. The seventh young woman –

the youngest and the most beautiful – was not crying. She was talking quietly to the others.

The seven princes were very surprised. 'Who are these young women?' said the oldest prince.

The youngest woman stood up quickly and she spoke to the others.

'Please stop crying now,' she said. 'Here are seven young men with horses. They will help us.'

'Why are you alone in this forest?' one of the brothers asked the young women. 'Soon, it will be night. Where are you going to sleep?'

The youngest woman spoke.

'Sir, we are princesses,' she said. 'Our father is a king. His kingdom is far away. Our mother is dead. When she died, our father married another woman. But his new wife, our step-mother, has always hated us.

'Our father has no sons,' the young woman went on. 'But our stepmother has a daughter of her own. She wants *that* daughter to rule our father's kingdom when he dies.

'When we lived at our father's palace,' the princess said, 'our stepmother made us work all the time. We were her servants. But she didn't want us to be servants. She wanted us to be dead! She wanted to kill us. She told our father many lies. At last, our father began to hate us too. Then our stepmother told some soldiers to kill us.

'A good servant at the palace heard our stepmother talking to the soldiers,' the young woman continued. 'He told one of his friends about the soldiers. The two servants helped us. This morning, they brought us here. But

'Why are you alone in this forest?' one of the brothers asked.

they said, "You must never return to your father's kingdom. We are happy to help you. But if your stepmother hears about this help, she will kill *us*."

'So now we have no home,' the princess went on. 'And we are frightened. Will you help us? If you take us to your home, we will be *your* servants.'

The young princes were sad. It was an unhappy story.

'Come with us, dear princesses,' said the youngest prince. 'We will take you home. Our father rules this kingdom. He is a good man. He will welcome you to his palace.'

So the eldest prince took the eldest princess on his horse. She sat in front of him. And the second prince took the second princess. Soon, each princess was sitting on a prince's horse. Slowly, they all rode back to the palace.

The king welcomed the young women to his palace.

'This is your home now,' he said.

Soon, all the young people fell in love. And soon, they were married. The eldest prince made the eldest princess his bride. The second prince made the second princess his bride. Each prince married a princess.

The youngest princess was called Balna. She was the bride of the youngest prince.

After a year, Princess Balna had a son. He was a beautiful baby. None of the other young princesses had babies. But all the princes and all the princesses loved Balna's little son. Everyone was very happy.

———

Two years passed. Life at the palace was peaceful.

But one day, Princess Balna's husband went hunting in the great green forest. He went alone. He did not return that night and he did not return the next night. The king was very worried.

On the third day, the young prince's six brothers went to the forest. They went to look for him. The six princes said goodbye to their wives.

'We will not return until we have found our brother,' they said.

A week passed, and the princes did not return. A month passed. Then six months. Still the princes did not return.

The seven princesses were very sad.

'Our husbands are dead,' they said.

2

The Wicked Magician

A year after the princes disappeared, a stranger came to the palace. He was a tall dark man. He wore a long black coat. He spoke to one of the guards at the gates of the palace.

'Will you take me to the princesses?' he asked. 'I am a *fakir* – a holy man. I can tell the princesses many secrets. I have news of their husbands.'

'Wait here,' said the guards. 'I will ask one of the king's servants to take you to the princesses.'

The guard told one of the king's servants about the fakir.

'Does he have some news about the princes?' the servant asked. 'If he knows where the princes are, the princesses will welcome him.'

The servant told the guards to open the gates. 'Let the stranger come in,' he said.

The stranger smiled. It was a terrible smile! The man was not a fakir, he was a magician! And he was a wicked man. His magic powers were evil. He had heard about the princesses. 'They are very beautiful,' people said. 'And all their husbands are dead.'

A servant took the stranger to the door of Princess Balna's room. Then the servant went away.

The door of the princess's room was open. The stranger stopped at the door and he looked into the room.

Balna was watching her little son. The little boy was sleeping, and the young princess was smiling.

Princess Balna was very beautiful. She was wearing a golden chain round her neck. A small picture of her husband hung from the chain. The princess took the chain from her neck and she put it round her little son's neck.

'This is for you, my son,' she whispered to the little prince. 'Remember your father!' And she smiled again.

Princess Balna watched her son. And the magician watched Princess Balna.

'I must marry her!' the magician thought. 'She must be

my wife!' He walked quietly into the room.

The princess looked at the stranger.

'Who are you?' she asked. 'Why are you here?'

The stranger smiled at the princess.

'Dear lady,' he said. 'I am a magician. I am the most powerful magician in the world. I know many, many things. I know everything!

'Your husband is dead, dear princess,' he went on. 'You must have a new husband now. You are beautiful. Please come with me and marry me. Be my wife!'

The princess was very angry.

'Go away!' she shouted. 'I love my husband. I love him if he is alive. And I love him if he is dead! I have a son. When my son is a man, he will look for his father. If someone has killed his father, my son will kill that man. I do not want to marry anybody else. Go away now! Go, or I will call the guards!'

But the magician was angry too.

'If you don't come with me, I will change you into a dog!' he shouted.

'I will never come with you!' said Princess Balna.

The wicked magician pointed at the princess and he said some words in a strange language. Immediately, the princess changed into a small black dog!

The magician took the dog in his arms and he quickly left the palace.

————

An hour later, Princess Balna's little son woke up. He started to cry. Balna's sisters heard him crying. They ran to

'If you don't come with me, I will change you into a dog!' the
magician shouted.

Balna's room.

'Where is our sister?' they asked themselves. 'She never leaves the little boy!'

They asked the servants about Princess Balna.

'Have you seen our sister?' they asked. 'Where has she gone?'

One of the servants remembered the tall dark stranger.

'There was a fakir here,' he said. 'He wanted to talk to Princess Balna. He wanted to talk to all of you. The fakir knew something about your husbands.'

The six princesses were very worried. The tall dark stranger had not talked to them. He had only talked to their sister.

'Someone has taken our sister away!' they said.

The guards and the servants searched the palace. They looked everywhere. But they did not find Princess Balna.

The king was worried too.

'I will give a bag of gold to the man who brings me news of Princess Balna,' he said.

But no one brought him any news. The king was very sad. A few weeks later, he died.

Princess Balna's little son became the king. But the eldest princess ruled the kingdom. She was going to rule the kingdom until the boy was old enough to rule it himself.

3

The Castle in the North

The young king was a fine, strong boy. He often asked people about his mother and his father. He asked his mother's sisters – his aunts – about his parents. And he asked his aunts about their husbands – his uncles.

'What happened to all of them?' he asked. 'Where did they all go?'

When he was very young, his aunts did not tell him the truth. 'All the princes died,' they said.

But when he was a young man of fifteen, one of his aunts told him the true story.

'Your mother disappeared when a stranger came to the palace,' she said. And she told the young king about the fakir.

'I will find her!' the boy said. 'I will find my mother and my uncles!'

So early one morning, the young king took his sword and he left the palace. He got on his horse and he rode away.

Day after day, he rode. He rode many hundreds of miles. He rode far to the north.

One night, the young king could not sleep. He was very excited.

'Tomorrow, I will find my mother!' he thought.

The next morning, he rode on. Far away, he saw the top of a high tower. The young king rode towards the tower.

'Will I find my mother there?' he asked himself.

In the afternoon, he came to a strange place. He came to the gates of a large garden. It was not a beautiful garden. The ground was dry and stony. And there were some big rocks standing inside the gates. In the middle of the garden there was a huge castle with a very high tower. It was the tower which the young king had seen in the morning.

The young man could not open gates of the garden. They were locked. But there was a little house outside the gates. The young king knocked at the door and an old women opened it.

'Sir,' the old woman whispered, 'you must not stay here! You must go away, quickly! It is very dangerous here!'

'Why must I go away?' the young king asked. 'Who lives in this strange castle?'

'A wicked magician lives in the castle,' said the old woman. 'He is a very evil man. He does not like people to come here. He changes them into rocks and stones.

'Do you see those seven big rocks?' the old woman asked. 'They were once young princes! One day, thirteen years ago, a young prince came here. The magician changed him into that rock by the gate. Soon afterwards, the prince's six brothers came to look for him. The evil magician changed them into rocks too! He has changed hundreds of men into rocks and stones!'

'Does the magician live alone?' asked the young king.

'Do you see that high tower?' the old woman said. 'There is a beautiful princess in that tower. She has been in there for twelve years. The magician wants to marry her but she will not agree to marry him. So he has locked the princess in a room at the top of the tower. The magician does not want any one to know about her.'

'My mother!' said the young king. 'The princess is my mother!'

The old woman was good and kind. The young king told her his story. He told her about his mother and his father and his uncles.

'Will you help me?' he asked her.

'Yes, sir,' she said. 'I hate the magician. I will help you. But it will be very dangerous.'

The old woman took the young king into her house. She found some girl's clothes and she told the young man to put them on.

'When the magician returns, he will come to see me,' the old woman said. 'He will ask me who you are. You must be my niece – my youngest sister's daughter.'

The next day, the magician came to the old woman's house.

'Has anyone come to the castle?' he asked her. Then he saw the young king.

'Who is this girl?' he asked.

'She is my niece,' the woman said. 'She has come to visit me.'

The magician looked at the young man. Then he spoke. His voice was soft and kind.

'Please do something for me, young woman,' the magician said. 'Please pick some flowers and take them to the beautiful princess who lives in the tower. Please do this

'The magician has locked the princess in a room at the top of that tower,' the old woman said.

every day. The princess will not speak to me, but she will speak to you. Tell her, "The flowers are a gift from the man who loves you." Will you do that?'

'Yes, I will!' said the young king.

The young king was excited. At last, he was going to see his mother. Quickly, he picked some flowers. Then he took off the gold chain which he wore round his neck. It was a beautiful chain. It had belonged to his mother. There was a small picture of his father hanging from the chain.

The young king tied the chain around the flowers. Then he walked across the dry, stony ground towards the tower. A guard opened the door of the tower and the young man started to walk up the stairs. Up and up he walked. At last he reached the top of the tower.

In a small room, he saw a woman. He gave her the flowers.

'Please take these flowers,' he said. But he did not say anything about the magician.

The woman looked at the young king. Then she looked at the flowers. She saw the golden chain with the small picture hanging from it. She looked at the young man again.

'Who are you, girl?' she asked. 'Where did you get this chain?'

For a moment, the young king could not speak.

Suddenly, the woman started to cry. 'The magician has taken my son too,' she said. 'Here is his chain. The magician has killed him.'

'No, mother,' said the young man. '*I* am your son. I came to find you. And I have found you at last.'

Mother and son were very happy. They told each other their stories. But soon the young king said, 'I must go now, mother. I will come again tomorrow. Soon, we will leave this terrible place!'

———

The next morning, the young king picked more flowers. He went to see his mother again.

'Mother,' he said. 'You must be kind to the magician today. You must talk to him. You must find out everything about him. Say to him, "I will never see my husband again. One day, I will marry you." Then ask the magician to talk about himself. I want to know everything about him. I want to find out how to kill him!'

In the afternoon, the magician came to visit Princess Balna. She spoke kindly to him. The magician was very pleased. He called his servants.

'Bring food and sweet drinks,' he shouted. 'We will have a celebration. We will eat and drink.'

The magician and the princess ate and drank. The wicked man was happy. Soon he was talking about himself. He answered all the princess's questions.

The princess remembered her son's words.

'Dear magician,' said Balna, 'my husband was a prince, but he was an ordinary man. He died. If I marry you, I want you to live for ever! Will your magic powers always protect your life? Will you ever die?'

'My life is protected by my magic powers,' the magician

replied. 'My heart is not here, in my body. My heart is hundreds of miles from here. My heart is in a small green bird. If someone attacks me here, they will not kill me. I will only die if the small green bird is killed. My enemies do not know this, so they cannot kill me!'

'And tell me, dear magician,' said the princess, 'where is the small green bird?'

'Far away, there is a great dark forest,' the magician answered. 'In the middle of the forest, there are six palm trees. The trees make a circle. In the middle of the circle of palms trees, there is a clearing. In the middle of the clearing, there are six barrels. The barrels are in a pile, one on top of another. The small green bird is in a cage. The cage is inside the barrel at the bottom of the pile.

'Twenty tall, strong men stand outside the clearing,' the wicked magician went on. 'These guards will kill anyone who goes near the palm trees. So, dear princess, my life is very well protected!'

4

The Small Green Bird

The next morning, the young king took more flowers to his mother. Princess Balna told him the secret of the evil magician's heart.

'I will find the small green bird, Mother,' the boy said.

'I will kill it. You will be free.'

'No! It is too dangerous, my son,' Balna said. 'Please, go home. Go back to the palace and leave me here. Go and help your aunts. Be a good king for your people. Take care of your kingdom and forget about me.'

But early the next morning, the young king left the old woman's house. He went to look for the wicked magician's spirit. Day after day, he rode towards the north.

———

One afternoon, the young king was sitting near a tree. Suddenly, he saw a snake. It was moving quietly along one of the branches of the tree. It was moving towards a birds' nest. In the nest there were two very young birds. They were eagles, but they were too young to fly. Their parents were not in the nest. They were hunting for food.

'The snake will kill the birds,' thought the young man.

Quickly, he ran to the tree and he killed the snake with his sword. He cut the snake in half.

Soon, the young birds' parents returned. They were very large eagles. They saw the dead snake. Quickly, they flew down and they thanked the young king.

'You saved the lives of our children,' one of the eagles said. 'What can we do to help you?'

The young king told the eagles about the palm trees in the forest.

'I have seen the palm trees,' said one eagle. 'Get onto my back and we will fly there!'

So the young king climbed onto the eagle's back and the bird flew up into the sky.

43

After many hours, the eagle flew down towards a great dark forest. In the middle of the forest, there was a circle of palm trees. The young king could see the clearing. He could see the pile of barrels.

The bird flew down to the ground. It landed in the clearing. The guards were standing outside the circle of palm trees. They did not see the young king until the eagle landed. Then, they started to run to the middle of the clearing. They screamed and they shouted.

Quickly, the young man pushed the barrels to the ground. Under the last barrel, he found the cage.

The young king picked up the cage. The small green bird was inside it. The young man got onto the eagle's back again. And quickly, the eagle flew up into the sky.

'Please take me to the magician's castle,' said the young king.

———

The eagle landed by the gates of the magician's castle. The young king sat on the ground and he took the small green bird out of its cage. The bird gave a loud cry.

And at that moment, the magician came out of the castle. He saw the young man with the bird. Suddenly, the magician was frightened.

'Young man,' he said, 'that is a very fine bird. Will you sell it to me? I'll give you a bag of gold.'

'I will not sell the bird to anyone,' said the young king. Gently, he put his fingers around the bird's neck.

'What do you want?' said the magician, softly. 'I have magic powers. I can give you anything that you want. I will

Quickly, the young man pushed the barrels to the ground.
Under the last barrel, he found the cage.

do anything that you ask.'

The young man pointed at one of the large rocks in the park.

'Change that rock into a man,' he said.

The magician said some words in a strange language. Suddenly, the rock changed into a tall man in fine clothes.

'Please give me the bird now,' said the magician.

'No!' said the young king. 'You must change *all* these rocks and stones into men. Then, I will give you the bird.'

The magician was very frightened. The young man knew his secret. The young man's fingers were round the small green bird's neck. If he killed the bird —

The magician said some more strange words. Soon there were hundreds of men in the park – kings and princes, young men and old men.

And then the young man killed the bird!

The magician cried out. He made a terrible sound. Then he fell to the ground. He was dead!

———

Soon, the young man rode home. His mother and his father and his uncles went with him. The young man's eldest uncle was the king now. The young man was a prince again. But he was very happy!

At last, they came to the palace. The prince's uncles saw their wives again after thirteen years. Soon there was a great celebration. And the celebration went on for thirteen days and thirteen nights!

'Please give me the bird now,' said the magician.

The celebration went on for thirteen days
and thirteen nights!

LOVE CONQUERS DEATH

Long ago, there was a great king in India. His beautiful palace was in a fine city. The king was a good ruler. He took care of his people. And the people in his country were happy.

The king and his wife wanted a child. For many years they waited for a child. Every day, they prayed to the Lord Brahma.

At last, the king's wife had a daughter. They called the child Savitri, because that was the name of the Lord Brahma's wife.

Savitri grew up, and she became a very beautiful young woman.

One day, the king spoke to his daughter.

'Savitri, you must get married soon,' he said. 'But I will not choose a husband for you. You must choose a husband for yourself. Tomorrow, you must go on a journey. You must visit the palaces of the other kings in this land. There are many handsome princes in India. Choose one of them to be your husband.'

———

The next morning, Savitri left her father's palace. She took four young ladies with her. They were her attendants for the journey.

Savitri and her attendants got into the king's golden chariot. Two beautiful white horses pulled the chariot through the streets. Soon, Savitri and her attendants had left the city. After an hour, they entered a great forest.

'Many good, holy people live in this forest,' said Savitri. 'Many good people leave their fines homes in the cities. They come to live here. They live in wooden houses. They live simply. They think about life and death. They pray to the gods. Many of the men here are hermits – they live alone. And many women come here to live together in an *ashram*.

'I will look for a husband in these woods,' Savitri continued. 'I do not want to marry a rich man. I want to marry a wise man. I want to marry a man who loves the gods. I want to marry a man who loves life and does not fear death.'

A few hours later, Savitri stopped the chariot outside a small wooden house. Savitri got out of the chariot and she went into the house. Inside, she saw an old man. He was praying to the gods. He heard Savitri coming into the house. But he could not see her – he was blind.

'You are welcome, dear lady,' the old man said.

'I thank you, sir,' said Savitri. 'Will you talk with me for a hour? Please, tell me about yourself. And tell me about your life in the forest.'

So the old man told Savitri about his life.

'I was a king,' he said. 'I ruled the kingdom of the Shalwas. I loved my people and they loved me. But one day, I became blind. An enemy attacked my palace. He took my kingdom. He is a cruel man and he is not a good king. The people do not love him.

'My enemy's soldiers brought me to this forest,' the old

50

man went on. 'If I return to my own land, they will kill me. So I live here with my son, Satyavan. We are poor now and we live simply. But we are happy.'

At that moment, a young man came into the little house. He looked at Savitri and she looked at him. And at that moment, they fell in love.

'This is the man that I will marry,' thought Savitri.

'You are welcome, dear lady,' the young man said. 'I am Satyavan. I live here with my dear father.

'There is an ashram near this house,' Satyavan continued. 'If you are tired after your journey, you and your attendants will be welcome at the ashram.'

'Thank you, sir,' said Savitri. 'We will stay at the ashram tonight.'

'I will take you there,' said Satyavan. 'The ladies who live at the ashram will give you food and drink. Please come with me.'

———

Savitri and her attendants stayed at the ashram for two weeks. Each day, Savitri talked to Satyavan. The two young people loved each other more and more.

One morning, Savitri spoke to the young man.

'Today, I will go back to my father's palace,' she said. 'I will tell him about you, Satyavan. My father will let me marry any man that I choose. He wants me to marry a rich man. But I will tell him about our love. He will let me marry you.'

So Savitri and her four attendants got into the golden chariot. They went back to the king's palace.

The two young people loved each other more and more.

The next morning, Savitri went to her father's room. The king was talking to a wise old man. The old man's name was Narada.

Narada was a holy man – a fakir. He loved the gods and he knew many things. He had been a hermit for many years. But now he lived in the palace. He was the king's adviser. If the king had a problem, he asked Narada for advice.

'Father,' said Savitri. 'I have found the man that I will marry.'

'Who is this man?' asked the king.

'He is a prince,' Savitri replied. 'But he is not a rich man. He lives in the forest. His name is Satyavan.'

Suddenly, Narada spoke.

'No!' he said. 'No! You must not marry Satyavan!'

'What is wrong?' asked the king. 'Do you know Satyavan? Is he an evil man?'

'No, he is not an evil man,' said Narada. 'He is a good, kind man. His father was the king of the Shalwas. When the king became blind, an enemy took his kingdom. Satyavan is a prince.

'But I know something more about Satyavan,' Narada went on. 'Before next year, Yama, the great Lord of Death, will come for Satyavan's spirit. Then the prince's body will die!'

Savitri was very unhappy. But she said, 'Father, I will be Satyavan's wife for a year. Then, if Yama comes for my husband, I will follow him. I will follow my husband to the end of the world!'

The king looked at his beautiful daughter.

'You must marry the man that you choose,' he said. 'You will marry Satyavan tomorrow.'

———

So Savitri and Satyavan were married. They went to live in the forest. They lived near Satyavan's father. They lived simply but they were very happy.

Then one day, Savitri and Satyavan were walking in the forest. It was nearly a year after their marriage. It was a beautiful, warm day.

Satyavan stopped walking. He said 'Savitri, my love, it is getting dark. I—'

And Satyavan fell to the ground. In a few moments, he was dead!

Suddenly, Savitri was very cold. She looked round and she saw Yama, the Lord of Death. His clothes were silver and his hair was black. But his eyes were red! His eyes were fire!

Yama was holding a silver rope. He had caught Satyavan's spirit with the rope, and he was pulling the spirit gently from the young prince's body.

'Savitri,' said the Lord of Death gently. 'You must say goodbye to your husband. I must take his spirit to my kingdom now.'

Then Yama took Satyavan's spirit and he started on his journey to the Kingdom of Death. And Savitri followed them.

When they came to the gates of Yama's kingdom, the

Savitri saw Yama, the Lord of Death.

Lord of Death stopped. He turned to Savitri.

'You cannot enter my kingdom,' Yama said. 'No living man or woman can enter the Kingdom of Death.'

'I will follow Satyavan,' said Savitri. 'I will follow my husband to the end of the world.'

'Savitri, you are a strong, holy woman,' said Yama. 'Ask me for a gift and I will give it to you. But do not ask for your husband's spirit. Satyavan is dead. He cannot live again.'

'Great Lord,' said Savitri. 'My husband's father is blind. I want him to see again. Give me that gift!'

Yama agreed to give Savitri this gift.

'The old king will see again!' he said. 'Now you must go back to the forest.'

'No!' said Savitri. 'I will follow my husband to the end of the world. I will come with you.'

Yama looked at the princess and he spoke kindly.

'Savitri, you are wise and good,' he said. 'Ask me for another gift. But do not ask for your husband's spirit.'

'Great Lord,' said Savitri. 'I want my husband's father to have his kingdom again. Give me that gift!'

Again, Yama agreed to give Savitri this gift. 'The old man will be a king again,' he said. 'And now you must go back to the forest.'

'No, Great Lord,' said Savitri. 'If Satyavan must die, I will die too.'

'Savitri,' said Yama, 'Satyavan cannot live again. I will give you one more gift. But do not ask for your husband's spirit.'

'Great Lord,' said Savitri. 'I want to be a mother. I want to have a hundred sons. Give me that gift!'

'You will have a hundred fine, strong sons,' said Yama.

'Then you must give me my husband's spirit!' cried Savitri. 'Great Lord, I will never marry another man. Only Satyavan can give me children. Only Satyavan can make me a mother.'

And Yama had to agree. The love of Savitri and Satyavan was stronger than the power of the Lord Yama. Love had conquered Death!

Yama gave Satyavan's spirit to his young wife. And Savitri ran from the gates of the Kingdom of Death. She ran to find her husband's body.

———

After that, Savitri and Satyavan lived for four hundred years. They had a hundred fine, strong sons.

Today, people still remember the story of Savitri. She followed her husband to the end of the world. She followed him to the gates of the Kingdom of Death.

Points for Understanding

1

1 Where did the brahmin live?
2 How many daughters did he have?
3 Why would no young man marry the daughters?
4 What was the jackal carrying in his mouth?
5 Who married the jackal?
6 Where did the girl and the jackal go to live?

2

1 Why did the jackal meet his father-in-law on the hillside?
2 What did the girl ask her father? What did he reply?
3 What gift did the jackal give to the old brahmin?
4 What happened a few days later?
5 What did the brahmin's neighbour sell in the market?
6 What did the neighbour take home with him?
7 Why was the neighbour surprised?
8 What did two of the brahmin's daughters find in the garden? Why were there not more of these things?
9 What was extraordinary about the things that the brahmin had sold to his neighbour?
10 What did the neighbour say to the brahmin?
11 Where did the brahmin go the next day?
12 What happened there?

3

1 Why did the jackal laugh?
2 What was the jackal's third gift to his father-in-law?

3 What did the jackal say to him when he gave him this gift?
4 Who visited the brahmin's hut? Why did he go there?
5 What did the brahmin tell this person?
6 What did this person take when he left the brahmin's hut?

4

1 Was the jackal happy when the brahmin visited him the third time?
2 What did the jackal give to the brahmin?
3 What did the jackal say about this gift?
4 The next day, the brahmin went out. Where did he go first?
5 How did the brahmin get the food jar?
6 Where did the brahmin go next?
7 'Where are my precious stones?' the brahmin asked. Who was he talking to? Where were the precious stones?
8 What did the jeweller give the brahmin?
9 Why did the jackal's wife follow her husband one morning?
10 What happened when they came to a lake?
11 What did the brahmin's eldest daughter find out?

THE WICKED MAGICIAN

1

1 How many sons did the king have?
2 Where did they like to go? Why?
3 'Something is wrong. Someone is very unhappy.'
   (a) Who heard the sound first?
   (b) Where did the brothers go?
   (c) What did they find?
   (d) Who was 'talking quietly'?

4 What had happened when this person's father had married a second wife?
5 How did a servant help? What did he say?
6 Who did the seven princes take to their home?
7 How did the princes take these people to their home?
8 What happened after the king welcomed the people to his palace?
9 Who had a baby boy?
10 Who went hunting alone?
11 'We will not return until we have found our brother.' Who said this? What happened?

2

1 Who came to the palace one year later?
2 What did he say to the guards?
3 Why did this stranger smile a terrible smile?
4 What did the stranger see when he looked into Princess Balna's room?
5 What did the stranger think?
6 What did he say to the princess?
7 What was her reply?
8 What happened to the princess?
9 Why did the eldest princess rule the kingdom?

3

1 'What happened to all of them? Where did they all go?'
   (a) Who asked this?
   (b) Who did he ask?
   (c) Who were 'them' and 'they'?
2 What did the young king find out when he was fifteen?
3 What did the young king say? Where did he go?
4 Describe the strange place that the young king came to.
5 Who did the young king speak to in a little house?
6 'Who lives in this castle?' the young king asked. What did he find out?

7 Who lived at the top of the tower?
8 Why was this person in the tower?
9 How did the old woman help the young king?
10 What did the magician ask the young man to do?
11 What did the young king take to the tower?
12 'Who are you, girl?' the woman asked.
   What happened next?
13 The magician was happy. Soon he was talking about himself.
   (a) What did Balna ask him?
   (b) What did the magician tell her?
14 What made a circle around the clearing?
15 What were piled one on top of another?
16 Where was the small green bird?
17 Who stood outside the clearing?
18 What did all these things do?

4

1 What did the young king tell his mother the next morning?
2 What did she reply?
3 How did the young king help the young eagles?
4 How did the young eagles' parents help the young king?
5 Where did the eagle and the king land?
6 Who was screaming and shouting?
7 What did the young king push?
8 What did he pick up?
9 Where did the young king go next?
10 Why was the magician suddenly frightened?
11 'I will do anything that you ask,' said the magician.
   (a) What did the young man ask?
   (b) What did the magician do?
12 What happened to the bird and the magician?
13 Who was the king now?

1 Who did the king and his wife pray to?
2 What did the king and his wife call their daughter?
3 What happened when their daughter grew up?
4 Who left the palace in a golden chariot pulled by two white horses?
5 Where did they go?
6 Who were hermits?
7 Who lived in an ashram?
8 What did these men and women do?
9 Who was the old blind man? What was his story?
10 Who was Satyavan?
11 What did Savitri tell her father?
12 Who was with Savitri's father?
13 What did Savitri learn from this person?
14 What did Savitri say about Satyavan when she heard this news?
15 Who had caught Satyavan's spirit with a silver rope?
16 Where was Satyavan's spirit going?
17 Savitri asked Yama for a gift. What did she ask for?
18 Yama gave Savitri a second gift. Why?
19 What was the second gift that Savitri asked for?
20 What did Yama say next? What did Savitri reply?
21 'Savitri,' Yama said. 'Satyavan cannot live again. I will give you one more gift. But do not ask for your husband's spirit.'
   (a) What was Savitri's reply?
   (b) What was Yama's answer?
   (c) What did Savitri say next?
   (d) Why did Yama have to agree?

ELEMENTARY LEVEL

A Christmas Carol *by Charles Dickens*
Riders of the Purple Sage *by Zane Grey*
The Canterville Ghost and Other Stories *by Oscar Wilde*
Lady Portia's Revenge and Other Stories *by David Evans*
The Picture of Dorian Gray *by Oscar Wilde*
Treasure Island *by Robert Louis Stevenson*
Road to Nowhere *by John Milne*
The Black Cat *by John Milne*
The Red Pony *by John Steinbeck*
The Stranger *by Norman Whitney*
Tales of Horror *by Bram Stoker*
Frankenstein *by Mary Shelley*
Silver Blaze and Other Stories *by Sir Arthur Conan Doyle*
Tales of Ten Worlds *by Arthur C. Clarke*
The Boy Who Was Afraid *by Armstrong Sperry*
Room 13 and Other Stories *by M.R. James*
The Narrow Path *by Francis Selormey*
The Lord of Obama's Messenger and Other Stories
by Marguerite Siek
Why Ducks Sleep on One Leg and Other Stories *by Anne Ingram*
The Gift From the Gods and Other Stories *by Anne Ingram*
The Land of Morning Calm and Other Stories *by Anne Ingram*
Love Conquers Death and Other Stories *by Catherine Khoo and
Marguerite Siek*
The Stone Lion and Other Stories *by Claire Breckon*
The Bride of Prince Mudan and Other Stories *by Celine C. Hu*

For further information on the full selection of Readers at all five
levels in the series, please refer to the Heinemann Readers
catalogue.

Heinemann English Language Teaching
A division of Reed Educational and Professional Publishing Limited
Halley Court, Jordan Hill, Oxford OX2 8EJ

OXFORD MADRID FLORENCE ATHENS PRAGUE
SÃO PAULO MEXICO CITY CHICAGO PORTSMOUTH (NH)
TOKYO SINGAPORE KUALA LUMPUR MELBOURNE
AUCKLAND JOHANNESBURG IBADAN GABORONE

ISBN 0 435 27325 6

The stories *The Gifts of the Jackal* and *The Wicked Magician*,
were first published by Heinemann Asia
(a division of the Reed International (Singapore) Pte Ltd
Consumer/Education Books)
in **Favourite Stories from India** by Marguerite Siek (1975)
© Marguerite Siek 1975

The story *How Love Conquered Death*
was published by Heinemann Southeast Asia
(a member of the Reed Elsevier plc group)
in **The Golden Legends Collection** by Catherine Khoo (1996)
© Catherine Khoo 1996

These retold versions by F.H. Cornish for Heinemann Guided Readers
Text © Reed Educational and Professional Publishing Limited 1997
Design and illustration
© Reed Educational and Professional Publishing Limited 1997
First published 1997

Illustrated by Kay Dixey
Illustrations and map, pages 6 and 7, by John Gilkes
Typography by Sue Vaudin
Cover by Haydn Cornner and Marketplace Design
Typeset in 11.5/14.5pt Goudy
Printed and bound in Spain by Mateu Cromo S.A.

99 00 10 9 8 7 6 5 4 3